GATHERING INFO

GETTING THE SCOOP BY USING YOUR WITS

by Tony and Jonna Mendez

Scholastic Inc.
New York • Toronto • London • Auckland • Sydney
Mexico City • New Delhi • Hong Kong • Buenos Aires

ISBN 0-439-90849-3

Copyright © 2007 by Scholastic Inc.

Designer: Aruna Goldstein
Illustrations: James W. Elston
Comic Strip Illustrations: Yancey Labat

Photos: Page 9: James Whitmore/Time Life Pictures/Getty Images.
Page 14: From the Public Domain. Page 15: International Spy Museum.

All rights reserved. Published by Scholastic Inc.

12 11 10 9 8 7 6 5 4 3 2 1   7 8 9 10 11/0

Printed in the U.S.A.

First printing, January 2007

Table of Contents

SNEAKIN' & PEEKIN'

A spy's job is all about information—finding it, sharing it, and keeping it safe. Need to know what your enemies are planning? Is there a mystery at school that needs to be solved? A spy needs to be able to scope out a situation, sense danger, and find out what's really going on—all while keeping the enemies clueless.

Wherever a spy goes, he needs to observe, remember, and analyze the most important things he sees. It may sound hard, but don't worry! With your latest **Ultimate Spy Club** handbook and spy kit, you'll learn about...

Observation & Surveillance

Sly spies rely on their surveillance skills to track the enemy, bring back critical info, and avoid being followed. Once you

learn the art of crafty observation, you'll be good to go when tracking down secrets.

Staying Secret

Having a cover story is a vital part of being a spy and getting info safely. Living your cover can make the difference between success and failure.

Elicitation

Most people love to talk about themselves. With some spy skills and a little patience, you'll have people spilling the beans in no time—so listen up!

And more!

Be sure to visit the
Ultimate Spy Club online at:
www.scholastic.com/ultimatespy

This month's secret password is:
getthescoop

What's in Your *Spy Kit*?

Look-Behind Glasses

These look-behind glasses have hidden mirrors in the lenses. Their rear-view optics will help you observe your target and analyze everything going on around you. You can adjust the mirrors so you never miss a thing. The next time you have a sneaking suspicion that enemies are approaching, they'll be the one in the dark!

MISSION #1:
EYES PEELED, EARS OPEN

A crafty spy is all about keen observation. Names, faces, places—it's enough to make a normal kid's head spin! But with a few spy skills, you'll know how to observe things closely and remember them well.

You don't need to mess with the enemy's stuff to collect your intelligence. You can gain info just by going different places—as long as you observe and remember what you see while keeping an eye out for threats to your operations.

You can learn to observe and collect intelligence just like a spy and learn to put that info to good use. You've got to be tuned in to what's going on around you so you're not left clueless!

Always Observing

Spying is all about observing the details of any situation. A lot of the time, in order to keep safe, spies have to work without any spy gear or secret notes. That means they really have to rely on their observation skills to get the info they need. Everything they see and do will have to be observed and remembered so they can recall it and report it in detail when they get back. Here are some fun exercises to help make sure you don't miss a thing!

Visual Sweep
Your most powerful observation tool is your eyesight. A spy can use his eyes to make a sweep from left to right and take in the whole area, memorizing details while he's sweeping the scene. It's like taking pictures with your eyes and your brain. Learning to do a visual sweep and notice details will help you detect any changes and collect all sorts of info in an instant.

Practice doing this with your room: Stand in the doorway and sweep the whole scene with your eyes. Take note of where specific things are located in the room as you make the sweep. If you notice something interesting, new, or out of place, make note of this as well.

Memorable Meeting

The next time you meet a new adult, try to pay extra attention to the details. Afterward, write down as much information as you can remember about that person. What was her name? Was she tall or short? How old was she? Did she wear glasses? What about her hair and eye color? Was she married? What job does she have? After a few times you'll start to pay a lot more attention to details when you meet someone new, and begin to mentally write them down. Your spy mind will be sharp as a tack!

The next time you enter a new class at school or join a new team, you'll figure out all those new names and faces in no time.

REAL SPY GADGETS

The Minox camera was a favorite of spies because it was small, easy to use, and took up to 50 pictures before the film had to be changed. It was a great camera to use when photographing the enemy's top secret documents.

Memory Mastery

One of the most important parts of gathering info is making sure you remember it. If a spy can keep the info in his head, he doesn't need to take notes—and that's a big help to security! Notes can get lost and wind up in the wrong hands. Learn these techniques and you can keep your memory strong and your spying stronger!

File and Don't Forget

Observing and recording info isn't done with just your eyes. All five of your senses can help you remember. If you learn something important, you can help yourself remember by storing it in as many different "files" in your memory as possible. If you see something and then say it to yourself, even silently, you'll automatically put it in 3 different places in your memory: the "seeing" file, the "hearing" file, and the "saying" file. That gives you 3 times as many chances to remember.

Mnemonics

Mnemonics are tricks that use associations with sounds and objects or memory "hooks" to help people remember things. Here are a few tricks you can use to help yourself remember.

➡ **Phrases.** Have you heard the phrases "Spring forward, fall back" and "Righty tighty, lefty loosey"? These phrases are designed to help people remember when to reset their clocks and which way to turn a twist-off lid. Try coming up with your own phrases to help you remember things.

➡ **Word Association.** When you're introduced to a new kid, you might try to use word association to remember his name. If a kid says, "Hi, I'm Sam," you might think to yourself, *Sam I am*—just like the character in the Dr. Seuss book! Lots of names can be remembered this way. Try it using some of your own associations.

➡️ **The Journey System.** You can use visual hints to help you remember things too. Say you're trying to remember a shopping list. If there are ten things on your list, visualize each item while you travel to the store. Visualize lettuce planted by the steps of your door, a glass of milk sitting on the mailbox, and a loaf of bread being eaten by the pigeons in the park. By the time you get to the store you'll be able to repeat the journey in your head and remember everything on your list.

➡️ **Special Sentences.** Another way to remember is to make up a sentence using the first letter of each item in a list. "Never Eat Shredded Wheat" reminds people of the 4 directions in order—North, East, South, and West. "Every Good Boy Does Fine" reminds musicians of the notes on each line of the musical staff—*E*, *G*, *B*, *D*, and *F*.

Regional Recall

This is a great exercise for anyone who wants to sharpen his or her memory: Sit down and try to make a map of your neighborhood. Draw a map of the block you live on, or

the apartment building you live in. Do you know the names of the people who live in the other houses or apartments? Do you know which people have dogs? Who has kids? What kind of cars people drive? See how many details you can recall. Being aware of these kinds of details will make you more aware of the things around you.

Party Practice

The next time you come home from a party, take a minute and see if you can write down a list of absolutely everybody who was there.

Don't leave anybody out! If you're not sure you've included everyone, ask one of your friends to check the list with you.

Surveillance

Surveillance is one of the main ways spies get information. It's what you do when you're following and observing the activities of your **target** without anyone seeing you do it. Maybe you need to figure out someone's schedule or find out what your friend wants for her birthday. Here are some tips to help you on your surveillance operations.

➡ **Eyes in the Back of Your Head.** Your look-behind glasses can really help you observe and gather info. They expand your field of view and let you see over your shoulder. No one will ever suspect what you're doing!

➡ **Doing the "Write" Thing.** A simple pad of paper and a pencil are excellent surveillance aids. If you're not in enemy territory, make brief notes to aid your memory. Your notes should be secure as long as they don't give away too many

REAL SPY GADGETS

Today, people use all sorts of satellites to collect information about what's going on down on Earth. Originally, a satellite system called **CORONA** sent info back to Earth by ejecting small canisters of film. The Air Force had to send planes to collect the canisters in mid-air with large nets. Imagine catching a butterfly with a butterfly net. Now imagine doing the same thing, except the butterfly is going hundreds of miles an hour, hurtling straight down towards the Earth, and the net is attached to a plane! Can you believe that they never lost a canister?

secrets. How many people are there? *3*. Where are they going? *N for North*. What time was it? *12:00 noon*. Well, 3N12 would mean nothing to anybody else, but it's all the info you need!

▷ **Making a SNAP! Decision.** A small, disposable camera can give you another set of eyes *and* another memory aid. A picture really is worth a thousand words!

▷ **Reflect on This.** Another simple gadget you can use on your surveillance mission is a small hand mirror. You can use a mirror to see behind you and even around corners. With practice, you can actually use a camera to take a picture of what you see in the mirror. But never forget to take a snapshot with your eyes and your brain first!

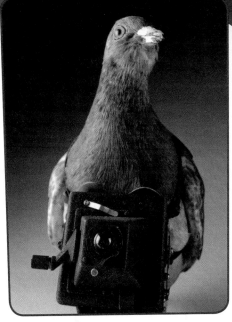

THE PIGEONCAM CAPER

Spies have always used tiny cameras in unusual ways, but the Pigeoncam Caper is probably one of the best examples of the extremes that the CIA will go to in order to get the perfect shot!

The CIA decided that homing pigeons could be great for collecting intelligence because they always return "home" (that's how they get their name). They decided to do a test to see if a pigeon could carry a very small camera on its chest. The engineers at the CIA created a small harness that would hold the camera securely but still allow the pigeon to fly. And guess what—it worked!

The next obstacle was figuring out how to tell the bird where the CIA wanted it to go. The scientists found that pigeons could be trained to follow a laser beam. If the scientists pointed their laser to a window across the street, the pigeon would fly to the window. Then scientists could remotely trigger the camera to snap a photo. Of course, the homing pigeon would always come back to where it started!

Bug in a Box

Trying to hear as much talk as you can is a great way to get info. Spies use all sorts of listening devices to help them secretly get in the know. A **bug** is a small listening device, like a microphone, that can be hidden almost anywhere. Here's a great way to make your own bug. Test your listening device and practice your bug-planting skills by asking a co-spy to let you listen in.

⇨ First, you need a set of walkie-talkies or a tape recorder and a box of your favorite snack.

⇨ Take the bag of snacks out of the box and put your listening device at the bottom. Next, take a pencil and poke a few small holes in the box near where the microphone is so the sound can come in.

⇨ Turn on your listening device. If you have a walkie-talkie in the box, you'll need to tape down the talk button. If you're using a tape recorder, press record.

⇨ Eat some of the snacks, and then put the partially empty bag back into the box. Now you have a perfectly innocent-looking, very sneaky listening device.

Stroll into your target's room. Look innocent! Ask your co-spy if he wants some of your snack. Take some yourself, and put the box down on a table. Make sure the microphone is pointed toward him. Then leave the room.

If you used walkie-talkies, you can leave the room and listen in using the other walkie-talkie. If you used a tape recorder, you'll have to go back into the room and tell them that you "forgot" your box of snacks. Then you can listen to the recording whenever you want.

SPY TIP:

All of these devices can help you collect information. Can you think of others?

In 1945, just after World War II and at the very beginning of the Cold War, Soviet "Young Pioneers" presented the U.S. Ambassador to Moscow with a large wooden carving of the Great Seal of the United States. The ambassador hung the seal in his office. Little did he know that there was a listening device hidden in the back of the seal! The bug transmitted important discussions to the Soviets for 7 years, until it was discovered in 1952 during a routine security check. It took a year and a half for scientists to figure out how the bug, which they referred to as "The Thing," worked.

Target Training

Is there a particular group of people you're interested in learning more about? Try using your spying skills to get as much information on these targets as possible. You might be surprised how much information is already available. Go to your school or home phone book. You can find out the address, phone number, and parents' names of anybody on your list. Next, get a local map and figure out where their address is. This might help you see if any of your friends live nearby, or better yet, know them.

Next, you might figure out if anybody you know is on your target's school bus or walks home the same way. You might arrange for one of your friends to bump into your target and start talking to him. Eventually, your friend can innocently ask the question you're interested in, and you can get the information you need.

This is the way that real spies work every day, all around the world. They need to find the right person and then figure out how to get the information they need from them.

Me and My Shadow

While conducting surveillance, it's important to make sure your operations go undetected. Spies must be able to tell if someone is following or **shadowing** them. Spies detect this kind of threat using a technique called **surveillance detection**. If you get a sneaking suspicion that someone could be watching you, there are important precautions you can take.

SDR

A **surveillance detection run**, or SDR, is one of the simplest and most important tricks a spy has to learn. It's the way you find out if the other guys are following you. Plan your daily activities and routes so you can always determine if you're being followed. Here's how it works:

⇨ **Who, Me?** Always look innocent, as if you're going about your usual business. If you keep looking over your shoulder or reversing direction, you'll look suspicious.

⇨ **False Stops and Starts.** Every so often you should change your route. Stop and sit in the park as if you're relaxing or waiting for someone. This will give you an opportunity to look around. You could also act like you forgot something or you've gotten lost. This will let you change direction so you can see if someone's behind you.

⇨ **Playing it Cool.** Remember to act natural and observe without looking like you're paying attention. Never make eye contact with someone who's watching you—just pretend not to see the person.

Cover-Up

Spies use **cover** to become invisible and hide in plain sight (cover for status) and to move to the area of interest without drawing attention (cover for travel). You'll always want to invent an extra-believable cover for use in your info-gathering operations, just in case you get caught in a place you shouldn't be. This excuse is called cover for action, and it had better be good!

Entering a store will force anybody following you to make a quick decision. Your cover for action—that you're going to go buy something—will force your follower to either come into the store or take up a position along the street to see you come out. When you leave the store you can take a free look to see if anyone's there.

POP Culture

In the movie *Cats and Dogs*, Mr. Tinkles uses the role of a fluffy kitty from a rich household as his cover for status while plotting to overthrow the dogs.

MISSION #2:
SPILL THE BEANS

The art of getting people to tell you what you need to know is another powerful tool in spying and gathering info. People know a lot of things that don't seem important but could be the key details you need to know. Getting people to talk without alerting them is called **elicitation**.

People love to talk, especially about themselves. All you have to do is be an eager listener and gently steer the conversation in the direction you're interested in. Asking people for help is another way to boost their egos. If you can make them feel important by asking for their help, they'll be glad to give you so much 411 it will make your head spin!

Getting the Gossip

Need the inside scoop on your new teacher? Want to know what fun clubs there are to join? One of the simplest and best ways to gather info is to meet people and become friends with them. If you seem interested, people will talk a lot. And pretty soon, they'll be telling you all sorts of things. Simply being a good listener is the most useful spy trait, and it also helps spies develop long-time friends.

Cover and Convo

It's not hard to make friends and build trust with a person if you can show genuine interest in their life story. Deep down, people want to share information with someone who seems trustworthy and caring. Asking questions about what a person does and how they do it is a good start, but asking how they feel about it is even better. If you can make eye contact, ask good questions, and focus the conversation on them, it can work wonders for your info gathering.

Here are some tips to help you in your elicitation operations.

➩ **Be Prepared.** Make sure you know what info you want before you get started. Draw up a list of questions you hope to answer.

➩ **Act Natural.** It's important to ask your questions in a way that sounds natural and won't let on what you're really after.

➩ **Make Eye Contact.** Making eye contact shows that you're paying attention and interested in what a person's saying. It also makes you seem more honest and trustworthy.

SPY TIP:

If you've ever played the game telephone, you know how mixed up info can get when it's passed through too many people. That's why it's always good to go straight to the source whenever you can.

SPY HISTORY uNCoVERed

Sometimes people who aren't professional spies are used for elicitation operations. During the Cold War, the CIA asked scientists to gather info at international meetings with foreign scientists. By doing this, the CIA found out that the Soviet Union was planning to put the first satellite, Sputnik, into orbit around the Earth. After the info was confirmed, President Kennedy called for the U.S. to be the first country to put a man on the Moon.

share information. After your info-gathering conversation, be sure to jot down any info you think you might forget.

 **Show Real Interest**. People naturally like to talk about the things they're interested in. If you can show an interest in what someone does or ask questions about the things they know about, they'll be much more eager to

➡️ **Ask Questions Cleverly.** Try to find different ways to ask questions that will make them seem more natural. Rather than asking, "Do you know Billy?" you could say, "My best friend goes to school with that guy, what's his name, Billy?" or, "I can't remember his last name, can you?" If you wanted to find out where Billy lived, you could ask what school bus he takes, or who he walks to school with.

➡️ **Get Help from Friends.** See if any of your friends know the info you're after. Or, if a friend of yours would have an easier time getting info from your target, have her do the first round of elicitation.

MISSION #3: DOING YOUR SPY HOMEWORK

Doing research is important throughout your info-gathering operations. In spy operations more intelligence questions are answered by researching and analyzing **open sources** like books, the news, and the internet than by busting into the enemy's secret headquarters.

If the research phase is done properly, it can also save you from all kinds of trouble. Sometimes agents find out that there wasn't a reason to spy on someone in the first place. Other times, having more info earlier could have made a huge difference by preventing something bad from happening.

Research & Recon

You'd be surprised how much info you can dig up by just going to your own open sources—magazines, books, the news, the internet, and your local library. Your local librarian is another great source of info because she is constantly asked a lot of questions. You can track down a lot of details on just about any subject.

Before Your Mission

One of most important times to do research is before an operation. Before you go on your mission and after you've done the initial research (**target analysis**), it's time to plan the details of your secret operation (ops plan). Even after the mission is over, you still

LIBRARY

may have to do a little extra research to fill in gaps in the data you've collected.

Different situations require different types of research:

⇨ **Surveillance Mission**. If your mission is going to be surveillance of a target, you need to know where your target lives, where he starts his day, and where he

POP Culture

In the movie *The Master of Disguise*, Pistachio Disguisey and his assistant are gathering info in a dumpster near where his father has been kidnapped. He uses special gadget glasses to help them find clues.

returns to every night. You need to know his pattern: How does he get to school—by bus, car, or subway? Does he travel alone, or with other kids? Does he go straight home? Does he know you? What classes does he take? Do you have friends in those classes? Do you have friends who know him? A sly spy will have all of the bases covered before he begins a mission.

⇨ **Cover Mission.** If your mission is going to involve a cover story, you need to get enough info to play the role. Not knowing the obvious things can be a dead giveaway. If you are pretending to be a photographer, you should know a lot about your camera and how to take good photographs. If you say that you're interested in baseball, then you should know some of the most important baseball statistics. A failure to have researched the backup information that matches your undercover identity can be a road to disaster. But if you can pass the test, it's an opportunity for some great info gathering!

SPY HISTORY uNCOVEREd

During the Cold War the CIA learned through observation and research how the Russian surveillance in Moscow was following U.S. officers. Because of this careful research, the CIA was able to plan and run operations without getting their sources caught. As a result, the CIA was able to collect lots of good intelligence about the Russians.

After Your Mission

After a successful spy operation, you're still not done! You have to analyze the data to produce **finished intelligence**. The fact that you have the inside scoop on the enemy should be a closely held secret. Guard it with your life!

These principles of spying can be used in your everyday life. Gathering information through observation and research will help you with everyday decisions. The key intelligence question might be, "What's the best place to research my homework assignments?" All important questions need good answers.

SPY HISTORY uNCoVERed

During World War II the Allies used their info-gathering skills by learning to read enemy codes and getting plenty of spies behind German lines. Through careful research and analysis of the info they'd gathered, the Allies knew where the Germans had their troops and how strong their defenses were. By giving them false information, the Allies were able to convince the Germans that they were going to attack somewhere else on D-Day. Because of their careful research and planning, the Allies won the battle.

SPY TIP:

Doing your research will also help you tell if someone is lying to you. A double agent is an agent sent by the enemy to give you false information. All info given to you by someone you don't really know should be double-checked through research.

Mission ACCOMPLISHED!

What you've learned in this book is the subtle art of collecting intelligence without ever making physical contact with the enemy. Your skills of observation, your ability to detect surveillance when you're gathering information, and your elicitation techniques guarantee that you can snag the snoops without breaking a sweat. The busybodies who are too interested in your biz are going to be tripped up by their own lack of spy skills. You have become one smooth operator, able to get the 411 without alerting 911, and leaving no trace. Way to go!

TONY AND JONNA MENDEZ
Writers & Consultants

Together, Tony and Jonna Mendez were spies who worked for the CIA for 52 years. Now retired, they have written two adult books about their careers: *The Master of Disguise* and *Spy Dust*. They live in Maryland with their 13-year-old son Jesse, their black Labrador named Pasquale Kostanovich Mendez, and a crazy, break-dancing cat named Figaro.

Glossary

These are the spy terms you need to know for continued undercover success!

Bug – A small listening device that can be hidden almost anywhere

Cover – A made-up story that a spy uses to blend in and keep the spying secret

Double Agent – A spy sent by the enemy to give false information

Elicitation – A technique used by a spy to get someone to talk and give info without realizing

Finished Intelligence – Intelligence info that has been well researched and is considered useful

Human Intelligence – Intelligence gathered with the help of a human source—HUMINT in spy slang

Mnemonics – A memory aid using the association of words, sounds, images, etc.

Open Sources – Places to gather info that are available to anyone, such as the public library or news media

Shadow – To follow someone

Surveillance – Any activity where someone is keeping track of another person's movements and activities

Surveillance Detection – Checking to see if you are being followed or watched

Surveillance Detection Run – A technique to check and see if you are being followed or observed

Target – A person or place that is the subject of an intelligence operation

Target Analysis – A process of researching and analyzing the nature of an intelligence target